WELCOME TO THE U.S.A.
NORTH DAKOTA

Written by Ann Heinrichs   Illustrated by Matt Kania
Content Adviser: Gregory S. Camp, PhD, Historian,
State Historical Society of North Dakota,
Bismarck, North Dakota

J917.84 Heinrichs

Published in the United States of America by The Child's World®
PO Box 326 • Chanhassen, MN 55317-0326
800-599-READ • www.childsworld.com

Photo Credits
Cover: Getty Images/The Image Bank/Michael Melford; frontispiece: North Dakota Tourism/Bruce Wendt.

Interior: AP/Wide World Photo/Minot Daily News/Kim Fundingsland: 30; Brand X Pictures: 6; Corbis: 9 (Layne Kennedy), 10 (Tom Bean), 18 (Dave G. Houser), 25 (Tim Thompson), 29 (Phil Schermeister), 33 (Joseph Sohm; ChromoSohm Inc.); Dakota Dinosaur Museum: 13; Minot Daily News: 26; North Dakota Tourism: 17 (Jason Lindsey), 21 (Barbara Stitzer); North Dakota Tourism/Dawn Charging: 14, 34; Fuller Sheldon/Fort Ransom State Park: 22.

Acknowledgments
The Child's World®: Mary Berendes, Publishing Director

Editorial Directions, Inc.: E. Russell Primm, Editorial Director; Katie Marsico, Associate Editor; Judith Shiffer, Assistant Editor; Matt Messbarger, Editorial Assistant; Susan Hindman, Copy Editor; Melissa McDaniel, Proofreader; Kevin Cunningham, Peter Garnham, Matt Messbarger, Olivia Nellums, Chris Simms, Molly Symmonds, Katherine Trickle, Carl Stephen Wender, Fact Checkers; Tim Griffin/IndexServ, Indexer; Cian Loughlin O'Day, Photo Researcher and Editor

The Design Lab: Kathleen Petelinsek, Design; Julia Goozen, Art Production

Library of Congress Cataloging-in-Publication Data
Heinrichs, Ann.
 North Dakota / by Ann Heinrichs.
  p. cm. — (Welcome to the U.S.A.)
 Includes index.
 ISBN 1-59296-478-8 (library bound : alk. paper)
 1. North Dakota—Juvenile literature. 2. North Dakota—History, Local—Juvenile literature.
I. Title.
 F636.3.H454 2005
 978.4—dc22   2005013658

Ann Heinrichs is the author of more than 100 books for children and young adults. She has also enjoyed successful careers as a children's book editor and an advertising copywriter. Ann grew up in Fort Smith, Arkansas, and lives in Chicago, Illinois.

About the Author Ann Heinrichs

Matt Kania loves maps and, as a kid, dreamed of making them. In school he studied geography and cartography, and today he makes maps for a living. Matt's favorite thing about drawing maps is learning about the places they represent. Many of the maps he has created can be found in books, magazines, videos, Web sites, and public places.

About the Map Illustrator Matt Kania

On the cover: This herd of horses calls North Dakota home.
On page one: Cross one of North Dakota's historic bridges into Valley City.

OUR NORTH DAKOTA TRIP

North Dakota's Nicknames: The Flickertail State and the Peace Garden State

Are you ready to tour North Dakota? Just follow that loopy dotted line. Or skip around and make your own tour. Either way, you're in for a great adventure.

You'll hang out with **pioneers.** You'll try on a buffalo robe. You'll learn how explorers lived in the wilderness. You'll see how a power plant creates electricity. You'll meet dinosaurs and prairie dogs. And you'll eat all the spaghetti you can hold!

Does that sound like your kind of fun? Then buckle up and hang on tight. It's time to hit the road!

WELCOME TO NORTH DAKOTA

As you travel through North Dakota, watch for all the interesting facts along the way.

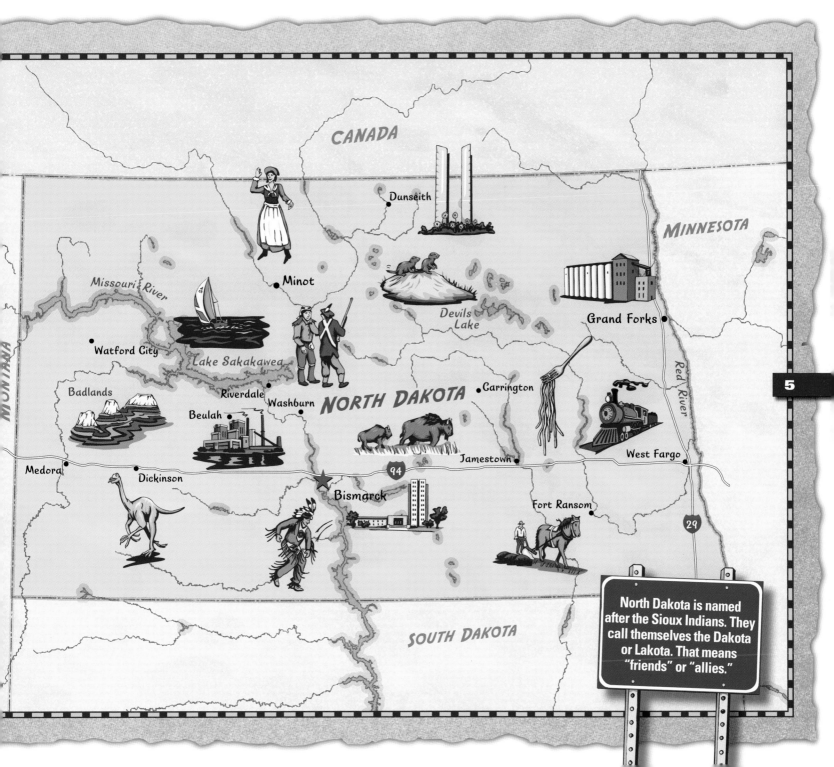

CANADA

Dunseith

MINNESOTA

Missouri River

Minot

Watford City

Lake Sakakawea

Devils Lake

Grand Forks

Badlands

Riverdale

Washburn

NORTH DAKOTA

Carrington

Beulah

West Fargo

Medora

Dickinson

Bismarck

Jamestown

94

Red River

29

Fort Ransom

SOUTH DAKOTA

North Dakota is named after the Sioux Indians. They call themselves the Dakota or Lakota. That means "friends" or "allies."

Painted Canyon in the Badlands

Do you like to hike? Head to the Badlands in Theodore Roosevelt National Park.

Painted Canyon will take your breath away! Just gaze at its rugged hills and rocks. They're striped in purple, green, yellow, and red.

Painted Canyon is near Medora in the Badlands. The Badlands run alongside the Little Missouri River. Their colorful rocks are worn into strange shapes.

North Dakota also has a big Missouri River. It winds through central and western North Dakota. The Red River is big, too. It forms the state's eastern border.

Fertile farmland covers much of North Dakota. In some areas, the land is almost flat. Other areas have gently rolling hills.

A point near Rugby is called North America's geographic center. It's the center of the continent when measured from north to south and from east to west.

Highest Temperature: Steele July 6, 1936 121°F (49°C)

Lowest Temperature: Parshall February 15, 1936 -60°F (-51°C)

CANADA

Pembina County

Wow! A pretty famous president enjoyed the Badlands! Theodore Roosevelt spent time here. He said this helped him become president!

Turtle Mountains

• Bottineau

The Turtle Mountains rise in northern North Dakota near Bottineau.

Rugby •

Devils Lake

• Devils Lake

Red River

MINNESOTA

Missouri River

MONTANA

• Parshall

Little Missouri River

Badlands

Theodore Roosevelt National Park

• Medora

White Butte

Steele •

Devils Lake is near the town of Devils Lake. It's North Dakota's largest natural lake. No rivers flow into or out of the lake. Its water is salty.

HIGHEST AND LOWEST POINTS
Highest: White Butte at 3,506 feet (1,069 m)
Lowest: Pembina County at 750 feet (229 m)

Theodore Roosevelt National Park is in the Badlands. It's named after the 26th president. He had 2 ranches in this area in the 1880s.

SOUTH DAKOTA

STATE FLOWER
WILD
PRAIRIE ROSE

STATE TREE
AMERICAN ELM

STATE BIRD
WESTERN
MEADOWLARK

CANADA

Turtle Mountains

MINNESOTA

Devils Lake

Chill out, Sparky! That's not a dog barking. It's only a prairie dog.

Badlands

MONTANA

North Dakota is home to flickertail squirrels. They're a type of ground squirrel. North Dakota is sometimes called the Flickertail State.

The National Park Service has 5 sites in North Dakota.

SOUTH DAKOTA

North Dakota has more protected wildlife areas than any other state.

Sullys Hill National Game Preserve

You'll love exploring Sullys Hill National Game Preserve. It's on the south shore of Devils Lake. You'll see herds of buffalo, or bison. You'll also spot some elk. They're a really big type of deer.

Lots of prairie dogs live here, too. They dig tunnels to make prairie dog towns. How did they get their name? Because they bark when danger is near!

North Dakota is home to lots of other wildlife, too. Moose live in the Turtle Mountains. Deer and antelopes graze across the plains. Smaller animals scurry through the woodlands and meadows. They include beavers, foxes, rabbits, raccoons, and skunks.

These deer call the North Dakota Badlands home.

Elk shed their antlers in late winter. The antlers begin growing back in the spring. By fall, they're fully grown.

The Buffalo of Jamestown

Wow! That's a big buffalo! Visit Jamestown to see it for yourself!

A female buffalo is pregnant for about 9 months.

Buffalo are often hard to spot. But you won't miss the one in Jamestown. It's taller than a two-story building! It's the World's Largest Buffalo. This one is made of cement. Still, it's mighty scary looking!

Nearby is the National Buffalo Museum. Real buffalo roam the surrounding hills. One is named White Cloud. She's a rare white buffalo. White Cloud is sacred to many Native American groups.

Millions of buffalo once grazed across the plains. But hunters pretty much wiped them out. Very few are left now. North Dakota has several protected buffalo herds. Many private ranches raise buffalo, too.

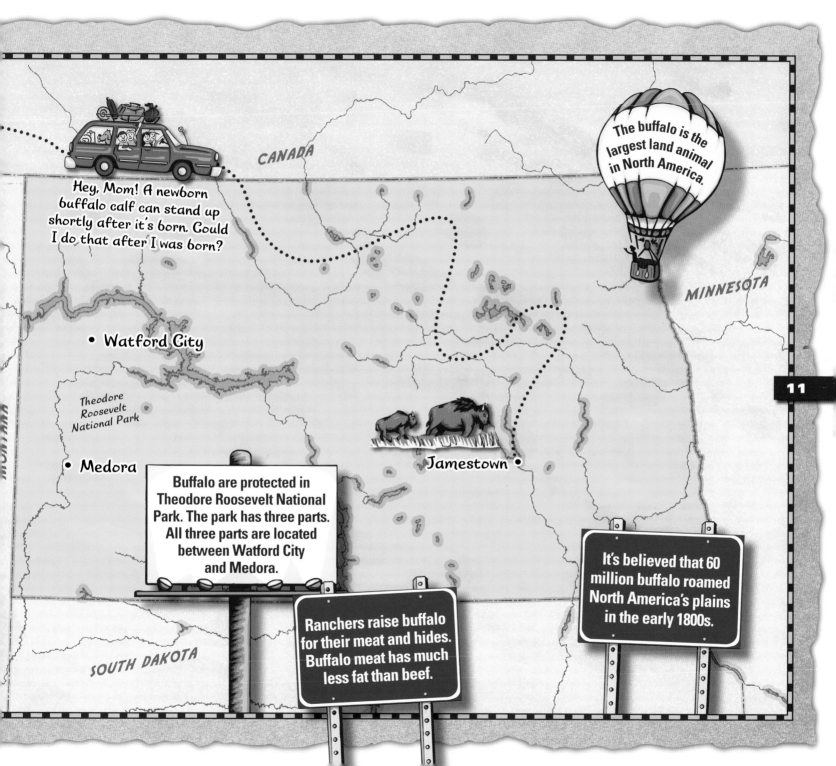

Hey, Mom! A newborn buffalo calf can stand up shortly after it's born. Could I do that after I was born?

CANADA

The buffalo is the largest land animal in North America.

MINNESOTA

MONTANA

• Watford City

Theodore Roosevelt National Park

• Medora

Jamestown •

Buffalo are protected in Theodore Roosevelt National Park. The park has three parts. All three parts are located between Watford City and Medora.

It's believed that 60 million buffalo roamed North America's plains in the early 1800s.

Ranchers raise buffalo for their meat and hides. Buffalo meat has much less fat than beef.

SOUTH DAKOTA

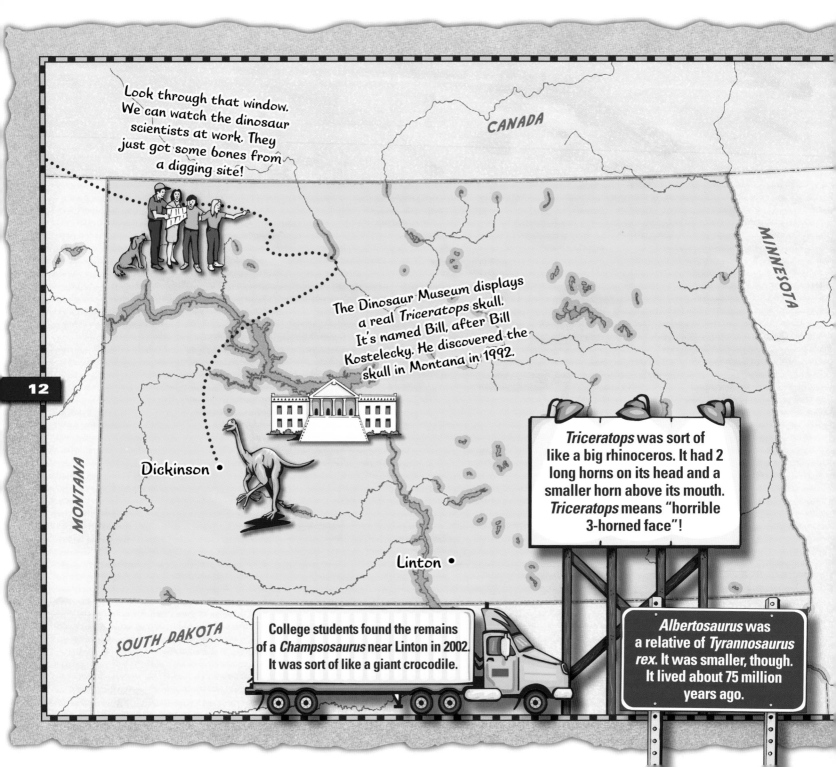

Dickinson's Dinosaur Museum

A big *Triceratops* guards the entrance. Are you brave enough to go in? You'll be glad you did. This is the Dakota Dinosaur Museum!

This museum has eleven life-size dinosaurs. Some are skeletons, and some are sculptures. Some have bony plates along their spines. Others have long, fearsome horns. One exhibit shows a nest of baby dinos. They're just hatching out of their eggs.

Watch out for the gigantic, meat-eating *Albertosaurus*. It looks very realistic! It's ready to chomp on a smaller dino. And that small dino is bigger than you!

Do you like dinosaurs? Check out the exhibits at the Dakota Dinosaur Museum.

Want to learn about Native American culture? Stop by the United Tribes International Powwow!

The Lakota Sioux were North Dakota's largest Indian group when white people first arrived.

The United Tribes International Powwow in Bismarck

Watch the dancers in spectacular costumes. Hear the deep throb of the drums. Taste some crispy Native American fry bread. It's the United Tribes International Powwow!

This is one of the nation's biggest Indian festivals. More than seventy Indian groups attend. They take part in dance and drumming contests. And they offer **traditional** foods and crafts.

Thousands of Indians once lived in North Dakota. Some lived in earthen lodges. Others built tepees covered with animal skins. They hunted buffalo across the plains. The animals provided meat and hides. Even the bones were useful. They were made into tools. Today, many Indians still call North Dakota home.

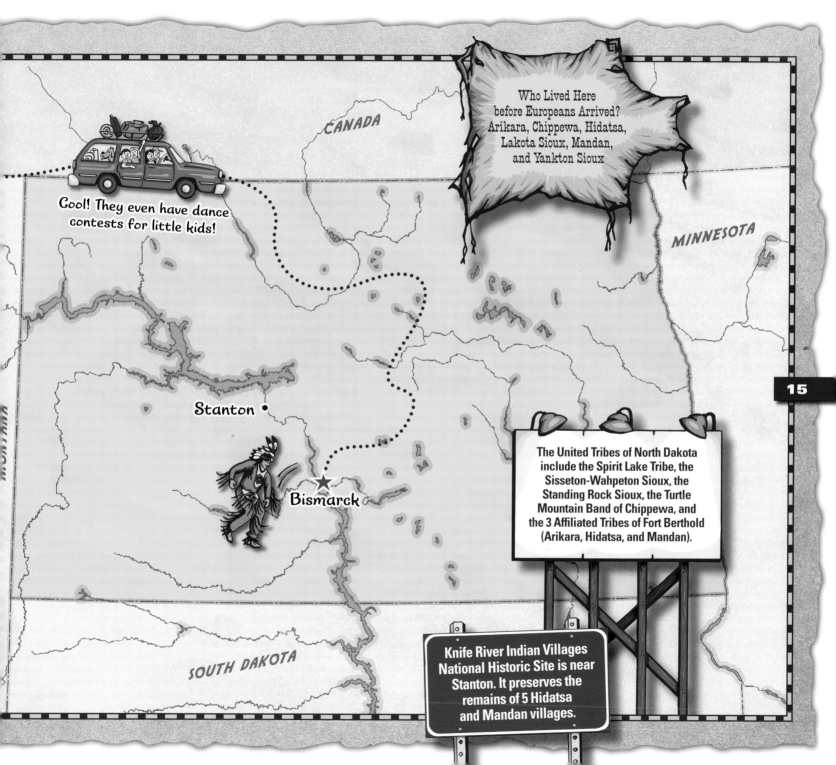

CANADA

MINNESOTA

Cool! They even have dance contests for little kids!

Who Lived Here before Europeans Arrived? Arikara, Chippewa, Hidatsa, Lakota Sioux, Mandan, and Yankton Sioux

Stanton •

★ Bismarck

SOUTH DAKOTA

The United Tribes of North Dakota include the Spirit Lake Tribe, the Sisseton-Wahpeton Sioux, the Standing Rock Sioux, the Turtle Mountain Band of Chippewa, and the 3 Affiliated Tribes of Fort Berthold (Arikara, Hidatsa, and Mandan).

Knife River Indian Villages National Historic Site is near Stanton. It preserves the remains of 5 Hidatsa and Mandan villages.

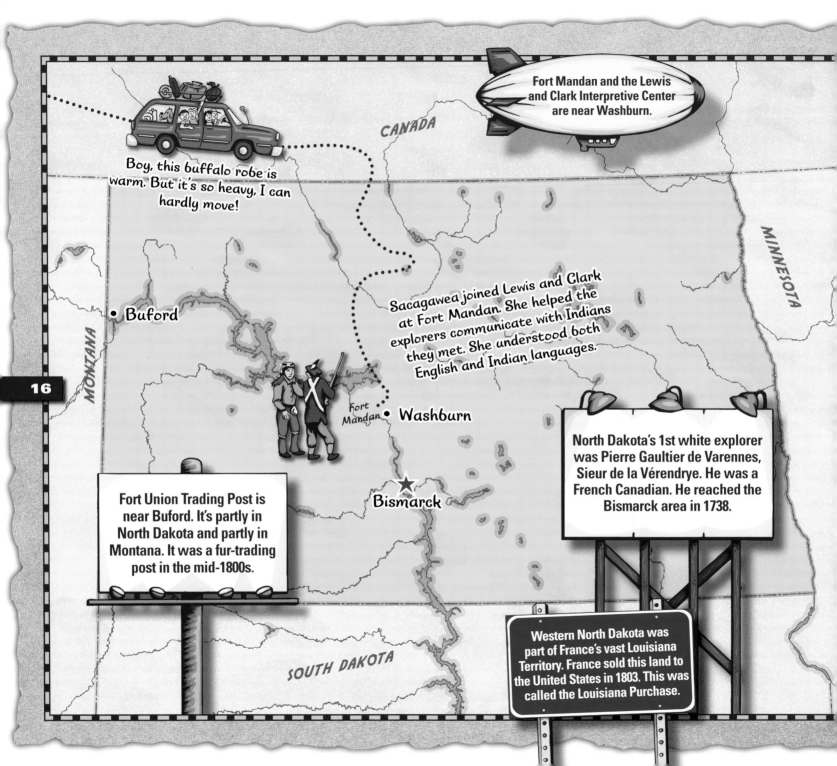

Fort Mandan and the Lewis and Clark Interpretive Center are near Washburn.

Boy, this buffalo robe is warm. But it's so heavy, I can hardly move!

CANADA

MONTANA

MINNESOTA

• Buford

Sacagawea joined Lewis and Clark at Fort Mandan. She helped the explorers communicate with Indians they met. She understood both English and Indian languages.

Fort Mandan

• Washburn

North Dakota's 1st white explorer was Pierre Gaultier de Varennes, Sieur de la Vérendrye. He was a French Canadian. He reached the Bismarck area in 1738.

★ Bismarck

Fort Union Trading Post is near Buford. It's partly in North Dakota and partly in Montana. It was a fur-trading post in the mid-1800s.

Western North Dakota was part of France's vast Louisiana Territory. France sold this land to the United States in 1803. This was called the Louisiana Purchase.

SOUTH DAKOTA

Lewis and Clark at Fort Mandan

Is this Sacagawea? No! Fort Mandan features costumed actors who reenact historical events.

Try on a buffalo robe. See a canoe carved from a tree trunk. Then try wearing a cradle board. Indian mothers carried their babies in these. You're exploring the Lewis and Clark Interpretive Center!

Next, visit nearby Fort Mandan. Explorers built a camp here in 1804. They were Meriwether Lewis and William Clark. Friendly Mandan people helped them survive the winter.

The United States gained this territory in 1803. President Thomas Jefferson sent Lewis and Clark to explore. Jefferson wanted them to reach the Pacific Ocean. And they did! They passed through North Dakota again in 1806.

France claimed the Louisiana Territory in 1682.

Behave yourself! Bonanzaville USA features a jail from pioneer days.

North Dakota was the 39th state to enter the Union. It joined on November 2, 1889.

West Fargo's Bonanzaville USA

How did North Dakota's pioneers live? Just visit Bonanzaville USA during Pioneer Days. Costumed folks show you how pioneers worked. They're making all they need by hand!

Railroads reached North Dakota in 1872. Then people could travel there easily. Big wheat farms opened in the Red River valley. They were called **bonanza farms.** Then thousands more settlers began pouring in.

Meanwhile, Indians were fighting to keep their lands. Lakota Sioux chief Sitting Bull fought bravely. He led many battles against the U.S. Army. He finally gave up in 1881.

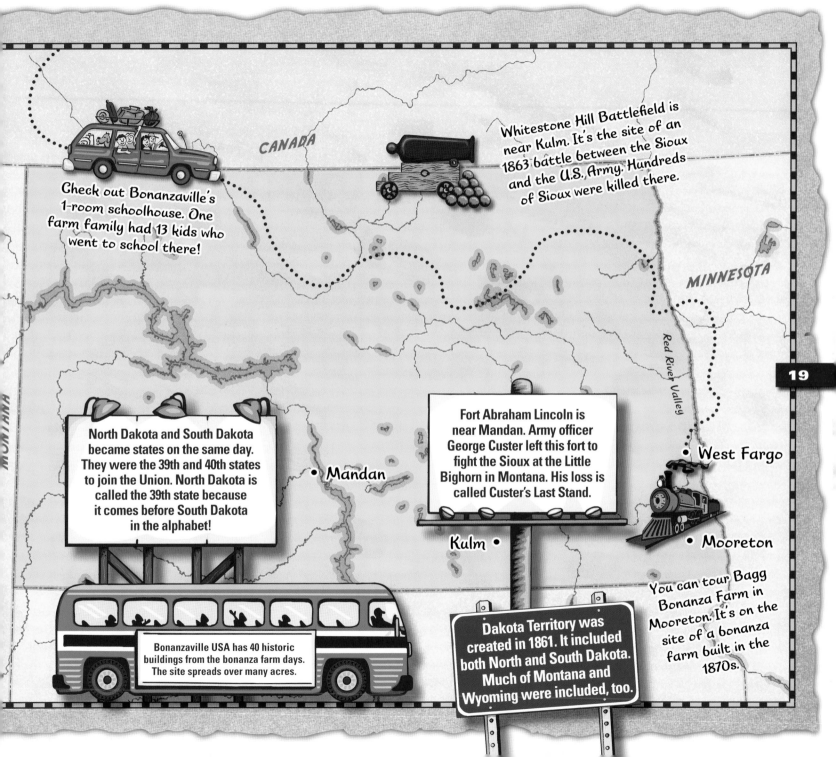

Check out Bonanzaville's 1-room schoolhouse. One farm family had 13 kids who went to school there!

Whitestone Hill Battlefield is near Kulm. It's the site of an 1863 battle between the Sioux and the U.S. Army. Hundreds of Sioux were killed there.

CANADA

MINNESOTA

Red River Valley

MONTANA

North Dakota and South Dakota became states on the same day. They were the 39th and 40th states to join the Union. North Dakota is called the 39th state because it comes before South Dakota in the alphabet!

Fort Abraham Lincoln is near Mandan. Army officer George Custer left this fort to fight the Sioux at the Little Bighorn in Montana. His loss is called Custer's Last Stand.

• West Fargo

• Mandan

Kulm •

• Mooreton

Bonanzaville USA has 40 historic buildings from the bonanza farm days. The site spreads over many acres.

Dakota Territory was created in 1861. It included both North and South Dakota. Much of Montana and Wyoming were included, too.

You can tour Bagg Bonanza Farm in Mooreton. It's on the site of a bonanza farm built in the 1870s.

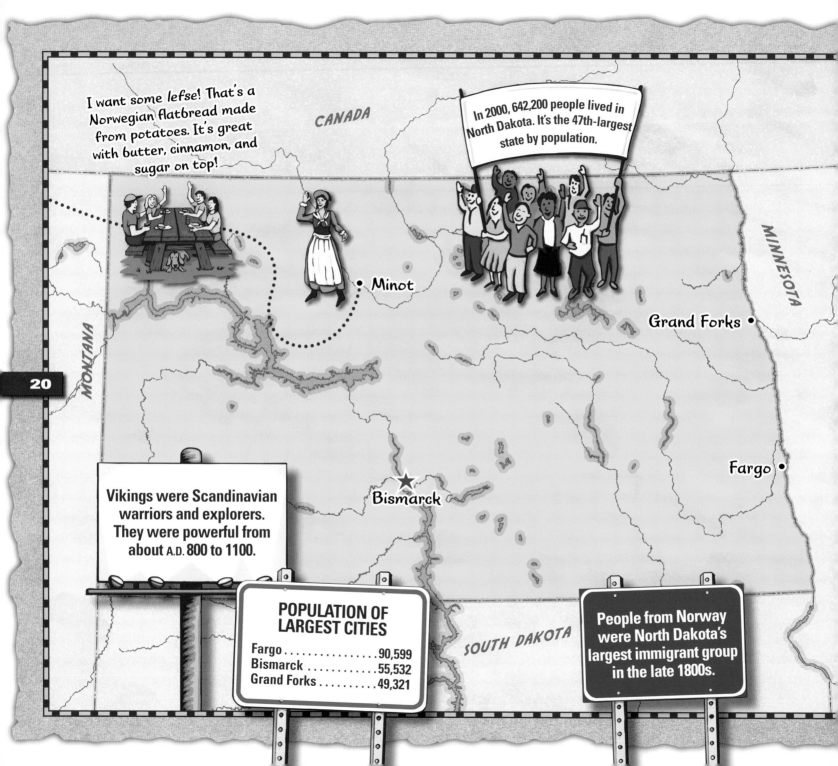

I want some *lefse*! That's a Norwegian flatbread made from potatoes. It's great with butter, cinnamon, and sugar on top!

CANADA

MONTANA

MINNESOTA

In 2000, 642,200 people lived in North Dakota. It's the 47th-largest state by population.

• Minot

Grand Forks •

Fargo •

★
Bismarck

Vikings were Scandinavian warriors and explorers. They were powerful from about A.D. 800 to 1100.

SOUTH DAKOTA

POPULATION OF LARGEST CITIES

Fargo 90,599
Bismarck 55,532
Grand Forks 49,321

People from Norway were North Dakota's largest immigrant group in the late 1800s.

Norsk Høstfest in Minot

Want to eat a Viking-on-a-stick? It's a meatball on a popsicle stick. It's dipped in batter and then deep-fried. Yum!

You'll sample this delicious treat at Norsk Høstfest. This event is North America's largest Scandinavian festival. Scandinavians have roots in Norway, Sweden, and Denmark. You'll eat some great food at the festival. You'll watch Scandinavian dancers and craftspeople, too. And you can even dance with a **troll**!

Thousands of settlers began arriving in the 1870s. They included lots of **immigrants.** Many came from Scandinavian countries. Others came from Germany, Russia, and Canada. They all worked hard to build new lives.

Strike up a tune! Scandinavian musicians play at Norsk Høstfest.

21

In 1915, 79 out of 100 people in North Dakota were immigrants or immigrants' children.

How did they farm without modern machinery? Find out at Sodbuster Days!

Minot Milling Company is a flour mill in Minot. It makes flour for pasta, pet food, pizza crusts, and tortillas.

Sodbuster Days in Fort Ransom

What was farming like in the old days? Just check out the Sodbuster Days festival. You'll see farmers grinding corn and sawing wood. Others are plowing fields and gathering crops. Horses and mules are pulling their equipment.

Farming is much easier now. Farmers use modern farm machinery. And much of it is made in North Dakota. Factories there make tractors and other farm equipment.

Foods are one of the top factory items, though. Some food plants make flour, pasta, or bread. Others prepare milk or make cheese. All these foods start out as farm products.

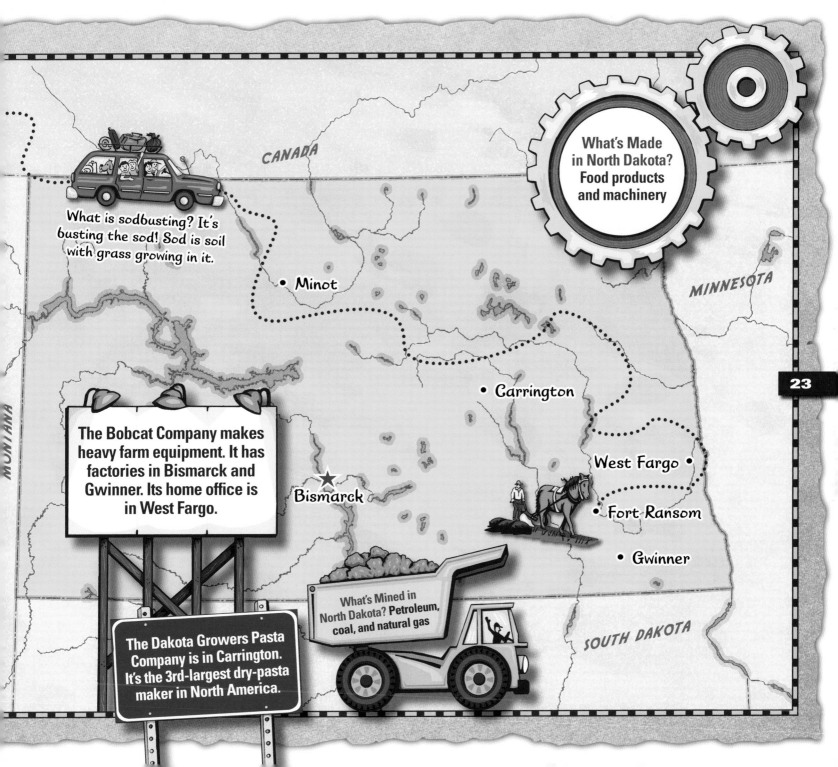

CANADA

What is sodbusting? It's busting the sod! Sod is soil with grass growing in it.

What's Made in North Dakota? Food products and machinery

MINNESOTA

• Minot

The Bobcat Company makes heavy farm equipment. It has factories in Bismarck and Gwinner. Its home office is in West Fargo.

• Carrington

★ Bismarck

West Fargo •

• Fort Ransom

• Gwinner

MONTANA

What's Mined in North Dakota? Petroleum, coal, and natural gas

The Dakota Growers Pasta Company is in Carrington. It's the 3rd-largest dry-pasta maker in North America.

SOUTH DAKOTA

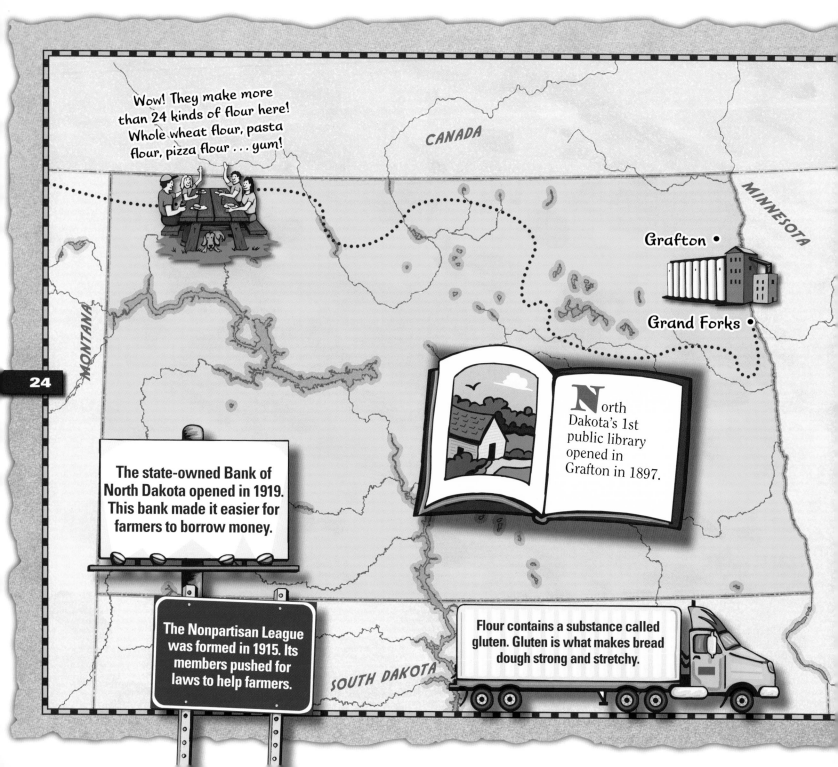

The North Dakota Mill and Elevator in Grand Forks

Want to learn how a mill operates? Head to Grand Forks!

Huge trucks drive in and out. The smokestack belches away. This enormous building is really busy! You'd never guess it's a historic site.

This is the North Dakota Mill and Elevator. It opened in 1922. And it's working harder than ever today. Its tall elevators store grain. And its mills grind wheat into flour.

North Dakota farmers were angry in the early 1900s. Big companies owned the grain-processing plants. They made lots of money. But the farmers made very little profit. They demanded help from the state. Soon the state-owned North Dakota Mill opened. It gave farmers good prices for their grain.

25

Yum, spaghetti! Get your fill at PastaFest!

Farfalle is a type of pasta that looks like a bowtie!

PastaFest in Carrington

Do you like foods such as spaghetti and macaroni? If you do, you'll love PastaFest. Just gobble away at the pasta-eating contest. Do you have any room left in your belly? Then head to the all-you-can-eat spaghetti dinner!

Wheat is North Dakota's major crop. Fields of golden wheat ripple across the plains. Most of the country's durum wheat grows there. It's used to make pasta. That's why there's plenty of pasta for PastaFest!

Farming is a big **industry** in North Dakota. Farms and ranches cover most of the state. Most farmers grow crops. But many raise beef or dairy cattle.

26

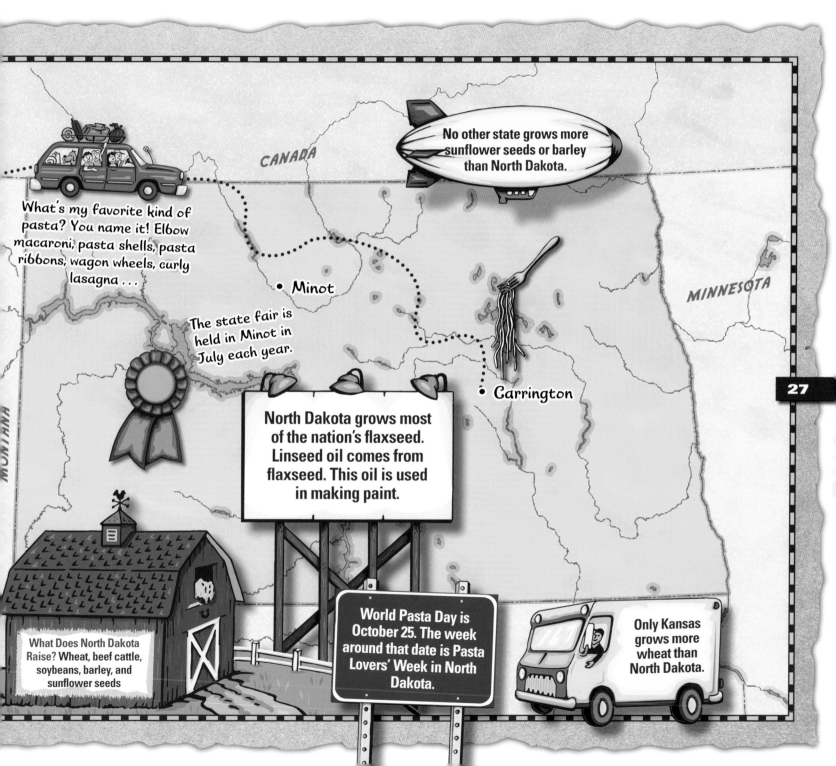

No other state grows more sunflower seeds or barley than North Dakota.

What's my favorite kind of pasta? You name it! Elbow macaroni, pasta shells, pasta ribbons, wagon wheels, curly lasagna . . .

CANADA

MINNESOTA

MONTANA

• Minot

The state fair is held in Minot in July each year.

• Carrington

North Dakota grows most of the nation's flaxseed. Linseed oil comes from flaxseed. This oil is used in making paint.

What Does North Dakota Raise? Wheat, beef cattle, soybeans, barley, and sunflower seeds

World Pasta Day is October 25. The week around that date is Pasta Lovers' Week in North Dakota.

Only Kansas grows more wheat than North Dakota.

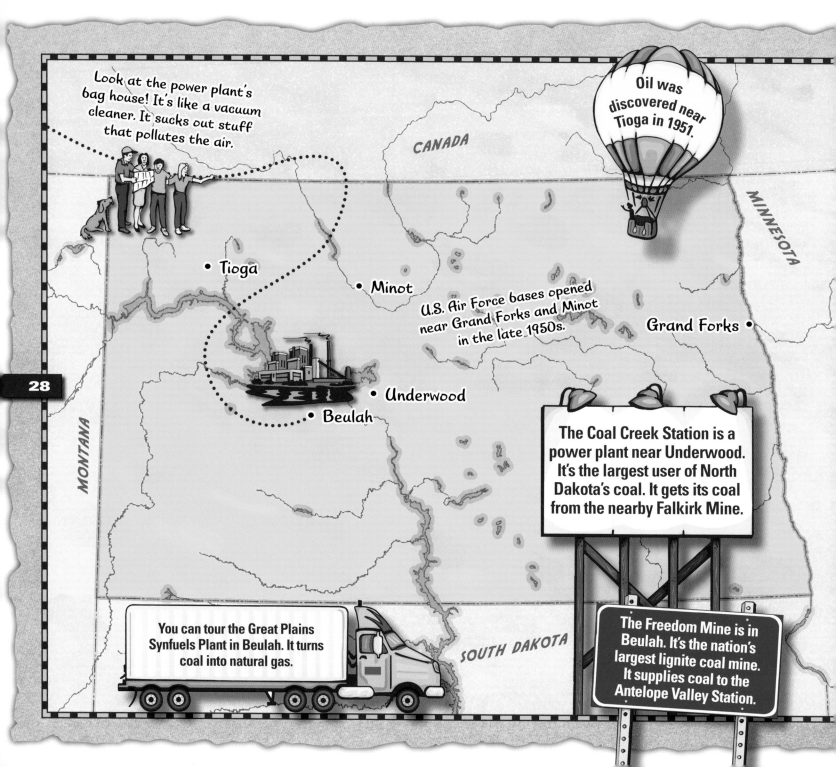

Antelope Valley Station

Tall pipes and towers rise above the plains. You've reached the Antelope Valley Station. It's a big power plant near Beulah. It burns coal to produce electricity. Step inside for a tour. You'll see its massive machines at work.

This power plant burns lignite coal. This type of coal is low in sulfur. When sulfur is burned, it produces sulfur dioxide. This substance causes air pollution.

North Dakota's mines clean their coal. They also repair land damaged by mining. The power plants help to protect the **environment,** too. The Antelope Valley Station cleans the gases it releases. Also, it doesn't release unclean water.

Interested in touring a power plant? Check out the Antelope Valley Station.

North Dakota has 7 power plants that burn coal to produce electricity.

Fun at Lake Sakakawea

Grab your fishing pole! Bring your life jacket! Lake Sakakawea offers all kinds of activities.

Hop in a boat and go fishing. Or maybe you'd like sailboating or windsurfing. There's plenty to do at Lake Sakakawea!

This lake is really long. Its east end is near Riverdale. Its west end is near the Montana border!

North Dakotans enjoy the outdoors. Some people head for the lakes and streams. Others like hiking through wildlife areas. Winter's great for ice-skating, sleigh riding, and skiing. Rodeos are popular events in North Dakota. So are Indian ceremonies. Many historic sites hold pioneer festivals. And there are farm fairs throughout the state. North Dakota has something for everyone!

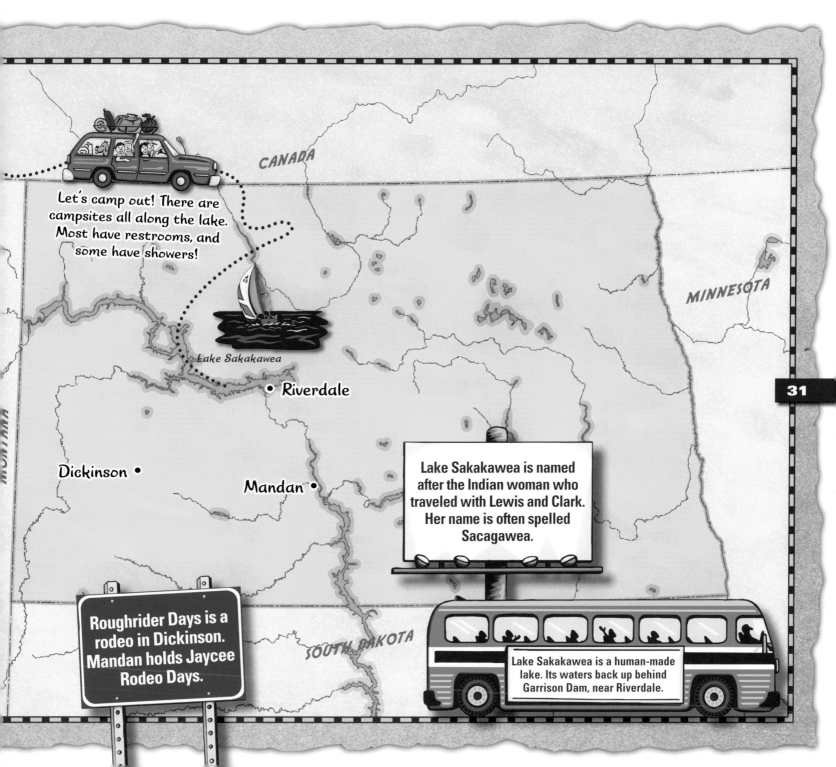

Let's camp out! There are campsites all along the lake. Most have restrooms, and some have showers!

Lake Sakakawea

• Riverdale

Dickinson •

Mandan •

Lake Sakakawea is named after the Indian woman who traveled with Lewis and Clark. Her name is often spelled Sacagawea.

Roughrider Days is a rodeo in Dickinson. Mandan holds Jaycee Rodeo Days.

Lake Sakakawea is a human-made lake. Its waters back up behind Garrison Dam, near Riverdale.

CANADA

MINNESOTA

MONTANA

SOUTH DAKOTA

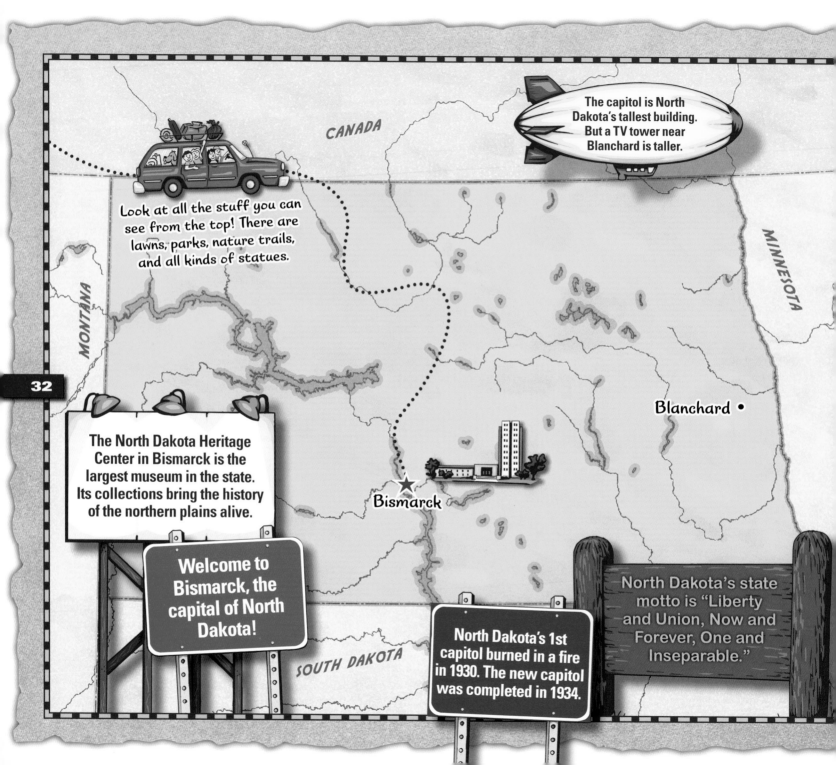

CANADA

MONTANA

MINNESOTA

SOUTH DAKOTA

The capitol is North Dakota's tallest building. But a TV tower near Blanchard is taller.

Look at all the stuff you can see from the top! There are lawns, parks, nature trails, and all kinds of statues.

The North Dakota Heritage Center in Bismarck is the largest museum in the state. Its collections bring the history of the northern plains alive.

Blanchard •

Bismarck

Welcome to Bismarck, the capital of North Dakota!

North Dakota's 1st capitol burned in a fire in 1930. The new capitol was completed in 1934.

North Dakota's state motto is "Liberty and Union, Now and Forever, One and Inseparable."

The State Capitol in Bismarck

What's the tallest building in North Dakota? The state capitol! It rises high over the plains. Just zoom up to the eighteenth floor. Then gaze out from the visitors' deck. What a view!

The capitol is North Dakota's state government building. The state government is divided into three branches. Each branch keeps a check on the others. One branch makes state laws. Its members belong to the Legislative Assembly. The governor heads another branch. This branch makes sure laws are obeyed. Judges make up the third branch. They study the laws. Then they decide whether laws have been broken.

The capitol is often called the Skyscraper on the Prairie.

Is it a skyscraper or a government building? Both! Head to Bismarck and see for yourself!

Three other states have skyscraper capitols: Florida, Louisiana, and Nebraska.

Want to take a scenic stroll? Be sure to tour the International Peace Garden.

The International Peace Garden

North Dakota is called the Peace Garden State. Why? Because of its **International** Peace Garden. This beautiful park is north of Dunseith. It's partly in North Dakota and partly in Canada. Canada and the United States built it together. It represents the friendship between the two countries.

Two garden areas are planted in flag designs. They look like the U.S. and Canadian flags. The floral clock is awesome. It's a working clock with flowers for a face.

Japan donated several tall poles to the garden. They say "May Peace Prevail" in twenty-eight languages. What a great message for us all!

About 150,000 flowers grow in the International Peace Garden.

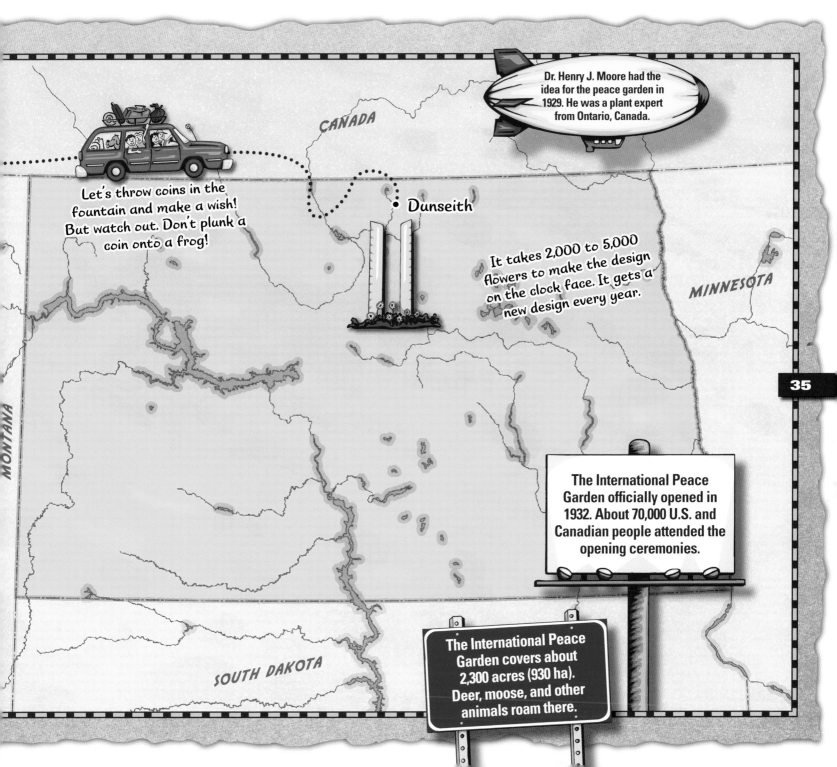

CANADA

Dr. Henry J. Moore had the idea for the peace garden in 1929. He was a plant expert from Ontario, Canada.

Let's throw coins in the fountain and make a wish! But watch out. Don't plunk a coin onto a frog!

• Dunseith

It takes 2,000 to 5,000 flowers to make the design on the clock face. It gets a new design every year.

MINNESOTA

MONTANA

The International Peace Garden officially opened in 1932. About 70,000 U.S. and Canadian people attended the opening ceremonies.

SOUTH DAKOTA

The International Peace Garden covers about 2,300 acres (930 ha). Deer, moose, and other animals roam there.

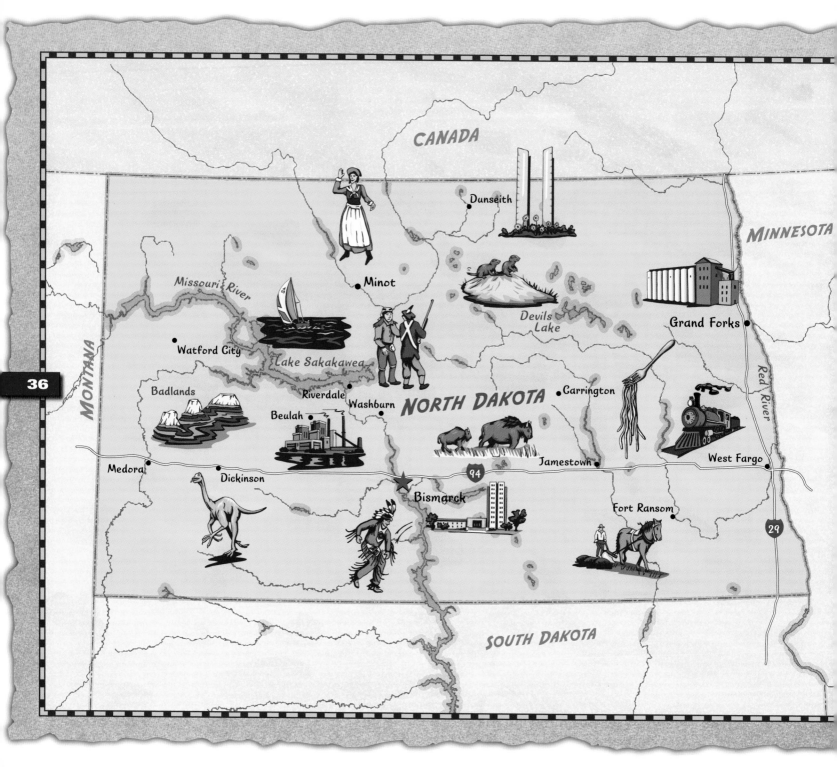

CANADA

MINNESOTA

Dunseith

Minot

Missouri River

Watford City

Lake Sakakawea

Devils Lake

Grand Forks

Badlands

Riverdale

Washburn

NORTH DAKOTA

Carrington

Beulah

Red River

MONTANA

West Fargo

Medora

Dickinson

Jamestown

94

Bismarck

Fort Ransom

29

SOUTH DAKOTA

OUR TRIP

We visited many amazing places on our trip! We also met a lot of interesting people along the way. Look at the map on the left. Use your finger to trace all the places we have been.

What is North Dakota's largest natural lake? See page 7 for the answer.

How many buffalo roamed North America in the 1800s? Page 11 has the answer.

What does the name *Triceratops* mean? See page 12 for the answer.

When was Dakota Territory created? Look on page 19 for the answer.

Which state grows more wheat than North Dakota? Page 27 has the answer.

When is World Pasta Day? Turn to page 27 for the answer.

What is North Dakota's capitol often called? Look on page 33 for the answer.

How many flowers grow in the International Peace Garden? Turn to page 34 for the answer.

That was a great trip! We have traveled all over North Dakota. There are a few places that we didn't have time for, though. Next time, we plan to visit the Children's Museum at Yunker Farm in Fargo. Kids can see the inside of a beehive, play with puppets, and study the stars! If there's time, visors can even ride the carousel!

More Places to Visit in North Dakota

WORDS TO KNOW

bonanza farms (buh-NAN-zuh FARMZ) large and profitable farms

environment (en-VYE-run-muhnt) natural surroundings such as air, water, and soil

immigrants (IM-uh-gruhnts) people who move to another country

industry (IN-duh-stree) a type of business

international (in-tur-NASH-uh-nuhl) relating to 2 or more nations

pioneers (pye-uh-NEERZ) the 1st people who settle in an unsettled land

traditional (truh-DISH-uh-nul) following long-held customs

troll (TROLE) a creature in Scandinavian folklore that lives in caves or hills

North Dakota covers 68,976 square miles (178,647 sq km). It's the 17th-largest state in size.

STATE SYMBOLS

State beverage: Milk

State bird: Western meadowlark

State dance: Square dance

State fish: Northern pike

State flower: Wild prairie rose

State fossil: Teredo petrified wood

State grass: Western wheatgrass

State honorary equine: Nokota horse

State march: "Flickertail March"

State tree: American elm

State flag

State seal

STATE SONG

"North Dakota Hymn"

Words by James W. Foley Jr., music by Dr. C. S. Putnam

North Dakota, North Dakota,
With thy prairies wide and free,
All thy sons and daughters love thee,
Fairest state from sea to sea;
North Dakota, North Dakota,
Here we pledge ourselves to thee.

Hear thy loyal children singing,
Songs of happiness and praise,
Far and long the echoes ringing,
Through the vastness of thy ways;
North Dakota, North Dakota,
We will serve thee all our days.

Onward, onward, onward going,
Light of courage in thine eyes,
Sweet the winds above thee blowing,
Green thy fields and fair thy skies.
North Dakota, North Dakota,
Brave the soul that in thee lies.

God of freedom, all victorious,
Give us Souls serene and strong,
Strength to make the future glorious,
Keep the echo of our song;
North Dakota, North Dakota,
In our hearts forever long.

FAMOUS PEOPLE

Christopher, Warren (1925–), statesman

Davies, Ronald N. (1904–1996), judge

Dickinson, Angie (1931–), actor

Dmitri, Ivan (1900–1968), artist

Eielson, Carl Ben (1897–1929), pilot

Erdrich, Louise (1954–), novelist

Flannagan, John (1895–1942), sculptor

Frelich, Phyllis (1944–), actor

Gass, William H. (1924–), philosopher and novelist

Jackson, Phil (1945–), basketball coach

Kittson, Norman (1814–1888), fur trader

L'Amour, Louis (1908–1988), novelist

Lee, Peggy (1920–2002), singer

Maris, Roger (1934–1985), baseball player

Oimoen, Casper (1906–1995), skier

Purpur, Cliff "Fido" (1912–2001), hockey player

Roosevelt, Theodore (1858–1919), 26th U.S. president

Rosenquist, James (1933–), painter

Sitting Bull (ca. 1831–1890), Sioux leader

Welk, Lawrence (1903–1992), television host

Woiwode, Larry (1941–), novelist

TO FIND OUT MORE

At the Library

Erdrich, Louise, Steve Johnson (illustrator), and Lou Fancher (illustrator). *The Range Eternal*. New York: Hyperion Books for Children, 2002.

Gayle, Sharon Shavers, Bob Dacey (illustrator), and Debra Bandelin (illustrator). *Teddy Roosevelt: The People's President*. New York: Aladdin Paperbacks, 2004.

Roop, Peter, and Connie Roop. *A Farming Town*. Des Plaines, Ill.: Heinemann Library, 1999.

Silverman, Robin Landew. *North Dakota*. Danbury, Conn.: Children's Press, 2003.

Sorenson, Margo, and Brian R. Austin (illustrator). *Tori and the Sleigh of Midnight Blue*. Fargo, N.D.: North Dakota Institute for Regional Studies, 2002.

On the Web

Visit our home page for lots of links about North Dakota:
http://www.childsworld.com/links

Note to Parents, Teachers, and Librarians: We routinely verify our Web links to make sure they are safe, active sites—so encourage your readers to check them out!

Places to Visit or Contact

North Dakota Tourism Division
Century Center
1600 East Century Avenue, Suite 2
PO Box 2057
Bismarck, ND 58503
800/435-5663
For more information about traveling in North Dakota

State Historical Society of North Dakota
612 East Boulevard Avenue
Bismarck, ND 58505
701/328-2666
For more information about the history of North Dakota

INDEX

Bye, Flickertail State.
We had a great time.
We'll come back soon!